PARIS

SHOPS & MORE

PARIS

SHOPS & MORE

Angelika Taschen
Photos Vincent Knapp

TASCHEN

HONG KONG KÖLN LONDON LOS ANGELES MADRID PARIS TOKYO

Croissant
pur beurre
0,95€

Nowhere in Europe is shopping such a delight as in Paris. Paris is the city of fashion and of luxury par excellence. Every French and international fashion label is represented here with a flagship store, many created by famous architects or designers, as was the Louis Vuitton store on the Champs Elysées, where numerous artists cooperated, including James Turrell, Olafur Eliasson and Vanessa Beecroft – a good way to combine fashion with art. But even just a stroll through Paris is a pleasure in itself, whether you saunter along elegant rue du Faubourg Saint-Honoré and stylish Avenue Montaigne, or walk through the alleyways of the Rive Gauche, where you will come across Christian Louboutin's trendy shoe shop, or the lingerie boutique Sabbia Rosa. But there are younger, up-and-coming places to visit, such as the concept store Colette, or Lucien Pellat-Finet's cashmere house, which sells pullovers in lively colours with knitted hemp-leaf patterns. If you've had enough of stylishness, go to Tati, the almost-cult bargain department store on Boulevard Rochechouart. And should you need a sit-down between shops, there are lovely cafés, bistros and restaurants everywhere – there really is no more delightful place to shop.

Nirgendwo in Europa kann man schöner shoppen als in Paris. Paris ist die Stadt der Mode und des Luxus par excellence. Jedes französische und internationale Modelabel präsentiert sich hier mit einem Flagshipstore; oft kreiert von berühmten Architekten oder Designern. Am Laden von Louis Vuitton auf den Champs Elysées haben auch zahlreiche Künstler mitgearbeitet, u. a. James Turrell, Olafur Eliasson und Vanessa Beecroft, so lassen sich hier sogar Mode und Kultur verbinden. Aber alleine ein Bummel in Paris ist schon ein Genuss, so flaniert man die elegante rue du Faubourg Saint-Honoré und die mondäne Avenue Montaigne entlang oder spaziert durch die Gassen der Rive Gauche, wo das szenige Schuhgeschäft von Christian Louboutin und die Dessousboutique Sabbia Rosa liegen. Es gibt aber auch jüngere Adressen wie den Concept-Store Colette oder das Kaschmirhaus von Lucien Pellat-Finet, der Pullover in grellen Farben mit eingestrickten Hanfblättern anbietet. Wem der Chic zuviel wird, der geht ins kultige Schnäppchen-Kaufhaus Tati am Boulevard Rochechouart. Und wenn man zwischendurch eine Verschnaufpause einlegen muss, gibt es überall hübsche Cafés, Bistros oder Restaurants – schöner shoppen geht wirklich nicht.

Nulle part ailleurs en Europe, faire du shopping n'est aussi agréable qu'à Paris, la ville de la mode et du luxe par excellence. Chaque marque française et internationale s'y présente avec un flagshipstore, souvent conçu par des architectes ou designers célèbres. Par exemple, de nombreux artistes, dont James Turrell, Olafur Eliasson et Vanessa Beecroft, ont travaillé au magasin Vuitton sur les Champs-Elysées, qui allie ainsi la mode à la culture. Mais c'est déjà un plaisir que de flâner dans les rues de Paris, de descendre l'élégante rue du Faubourg-Honoré, de faire du lèche-vitrines dans la très sélect avenue Montaigne ou de se promener dans les ruelles de la Rive Gauche, où se trouvent le magasin de chaussures très branché de Christian Louboutin et la boutique de lingerie Sabbia Rosa. Toutefois, il existe aussi de plus jeunes adresses comme le Concept Store Colette ou la maison du cachemire de Lucien Pellat-Finet, qui propose des pullovers de couleurs vives aux feuilles de chanvre tricotées. Enfin, si vous êtes plutôt en quête de bonnes affaires, rendez-vous chez Tati sur le Boulevard Rochechouart. Quand vous éprouverez le besoin de faire une pause, vous n'aurez qu'à vous asseoir à l'un des nombreux cafés, bistros ou restaurants. Existe-t-il une manière plus agréable de faire du shopping ?

Bon courage!

A. Taschen

Angelika Taschen

Palais Royal
Musée du Louvre

COMME
DES GARÇONS

Place
de la
Madeleine

Madeleine

Bd. des

Rue du Faubourg St - Honoré

HERMÈS

Rue de la Paix

Rue Royale

Bd. de la Madeleine

RITZ

CHANEL

Rue Cambon

Rue

Place
Vendôme

COM.
GARÇ

Place de
Marche
St-Honor

Ave. des
Champs-Élysées

Rue

Concorde

Rue

St - Honoré

Rue du Mont Thabor

Place
de la
Concorde

Rue

de

COL

MUSÉE DE
L'ORANGERIE

Tuileries

Quai

des

JARDIN
DES TUILERIES

MUSÉE
MODE ET DU T

Tuileries

Quai

Quai Anatole France

SEINE

Quai

Boulevard Saint-Germain

Rue de Lille

MUSÉE
D'ORSAY

Quai

Rue du Bac

Rue Saint-Dominique

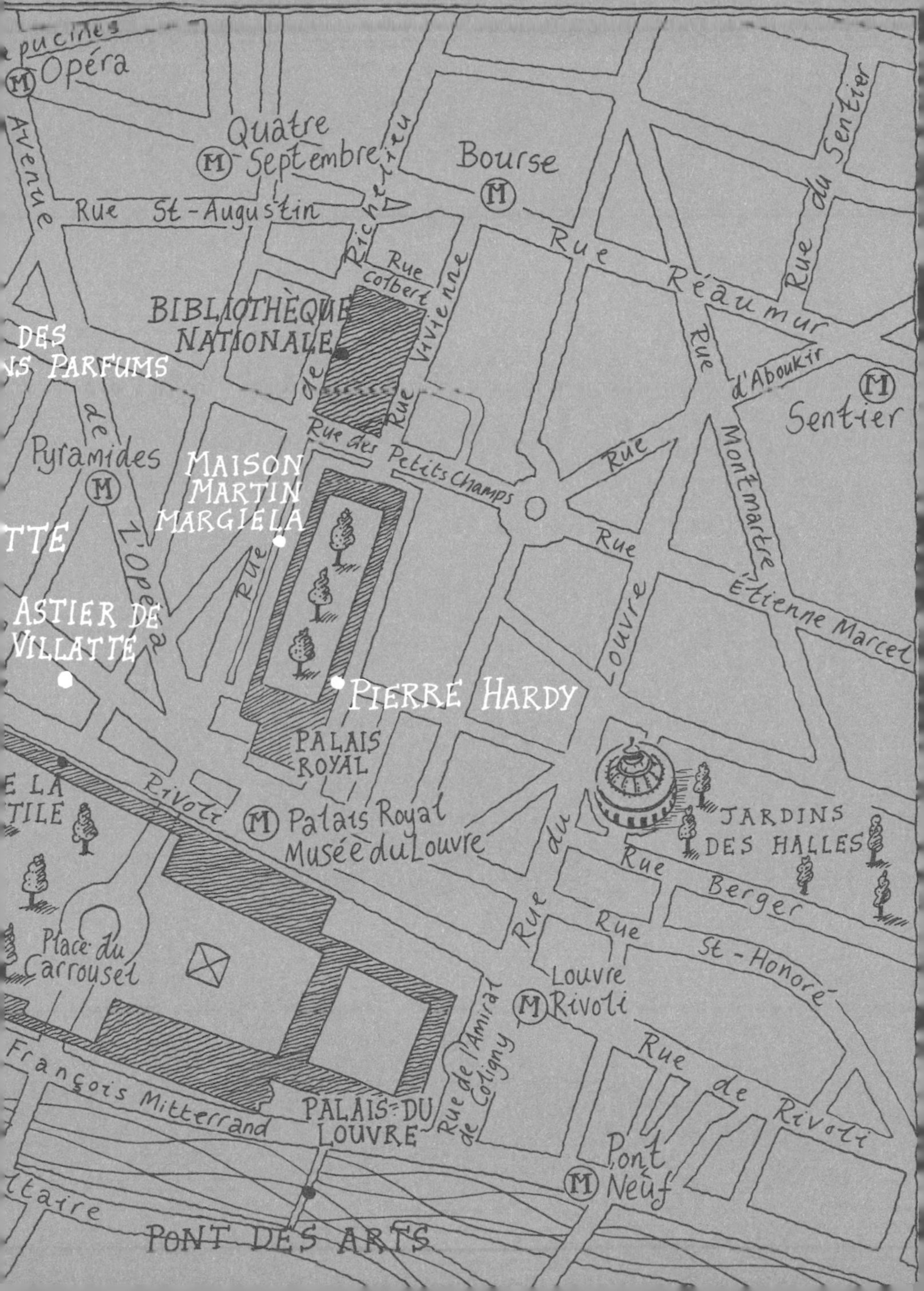

Opéra
Quatre Septembre
Bourse
Rue St-Augustin
Rue Réaumur
Rue du Sentier
Rue d'Aboukir
Sentier
Avenue de l'Opéra
Rue Colbert
Rue de Richelieu
Rue Vivienne
BIBLIOTHÈQUE NATIONALE
DES
NS PARFUMS
Pyramides
Rue des Petits Champs
MAISON MARTIN MARGIELA
TTE
ASTIER DE VILLATTE
Rue Étienne Marcel
Rue Montmartre
Rue du Louvre
PIERRE HARDY
PALAIS ROYAL
Rivoli
Palais Royal Musée du Louvre
JARDINS DES HALLES
Rue Berger
Rue St-Honoré
Louvre Rivoli
Place du Carrousel
Rue de l'Amiral de Coligny
François Mitterrand
PALAIS DU LOUVRE
Rue de Rivoli
Pont Neuf
PONT DES ARTS

Chanel

29–31, rue Cambon, 75001 Paris
☎ +33 1 42 86 26 00
www.chanel.com
Métro: Concorde/Madeleine

Colette

213, rue St-Honoré, 75001 Paris
☎ +33 1 55 35 33 90
www.colette.fr
Métro: Tuileries

NAGI NODA
Wall hanging stuffed animal of half deer.

F.U.N.
II

Comme
des Garçons
Parfums

23, Place du Marché St-Honoré, 75001 Paris
☎ +33 1 47 03 15 03
Métro: Tuileries/Pyramides

Astier
de Villatte

173, rue St-Honoré, 75001 Paris
☎ +33 1 42 60 74 13
www.astierdevillatte.com
Métro: Palais Royal Musée du Louvre

Maison
Martin Margiela

---

25 bis, rue de Montpensier, 75001 Paris
☎ +33 1 40 15 07 55
www.maisonmartinmargiela.com
Métro: Palais Royal Musée du Louvre

La collection pour femme

(6) Vêtements basiques pour femme

(10) Une garde-robe pour homme

Pierre Hardy

156, Galerie de Valois
Jardins du Palais Royal, 75001 Paris
☎ +33 1 42 60 59 75
www.pierrehardy.com
Métro: Palais Royal Musée du Louvre

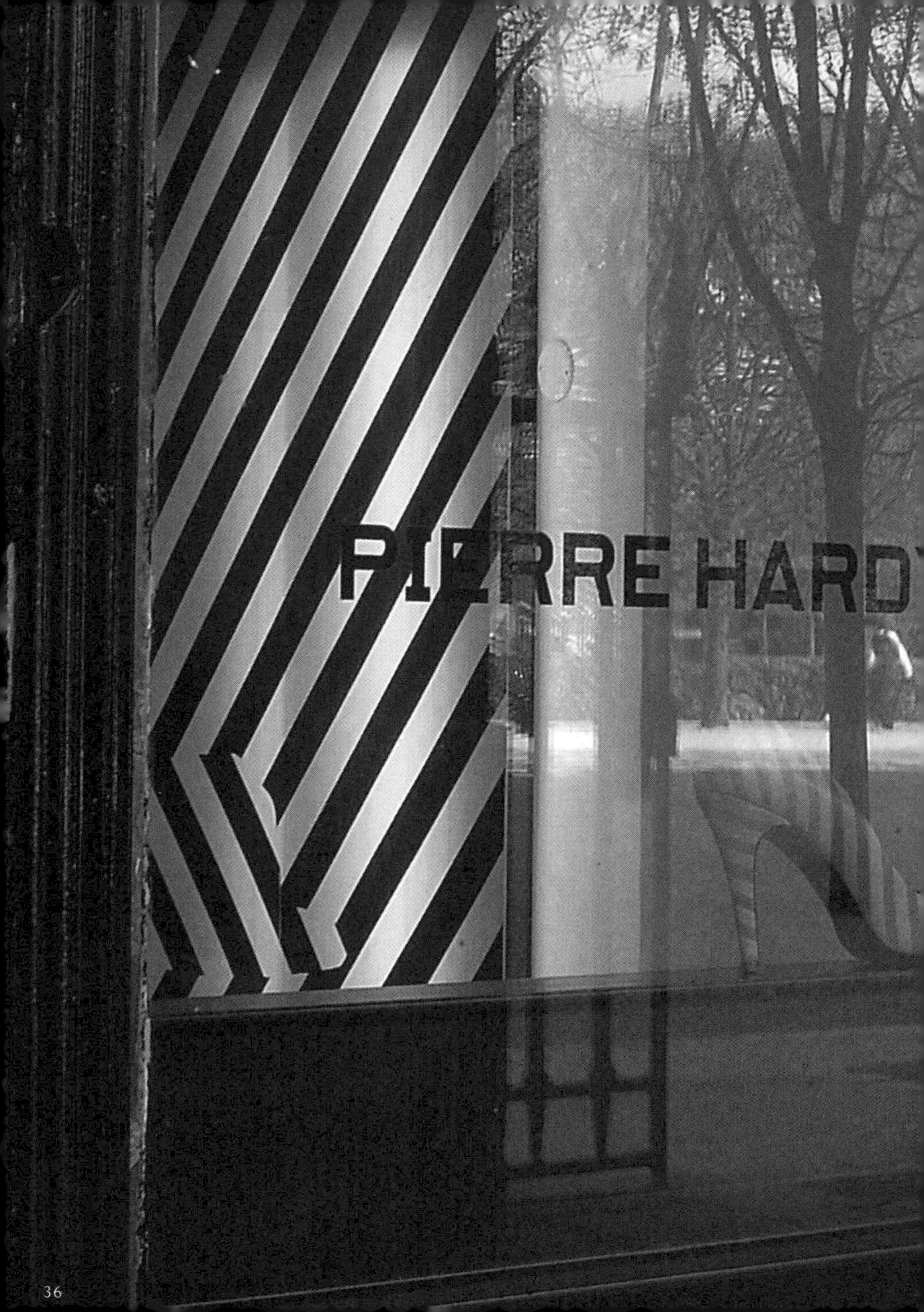
PIERRE HARD

Chanel
29–31, rue Cambon
75001 Paris
☎ +33 1 42 86 26 00
www.chanel.com

P. 12/13

Colette
213, rue St-Honoré
75001 Paris
☎ +33 1 55 35 33 90
www.colette.fr

P. 16/17

French Haute Couture
Design: Peter Marino (USA, 2003)

Open: Mon–Sat 10.00–19.00 | **X-Factor:** Coco Chanel opened her first atelier in this building.
"Fashion comes and goes. Style stays," said Coco Chanel and this conviction has been pursued here since 1910. The tweed costumes and Chanel No. 5 are legendary.

Öffnungszeiten: Mo–Sa 10–19 Uhr | **X-Faktor:** In diesem Haus eröffnete Coco Chanel ihr erstes Atelier.
„Mode geht. Stil bleibt", sagte Coco Chanel – diesem Credo folgt man hier seit 1910. Legendär sind die Tweedkostüme und „Chanel No. 5".

Horaires d'ouverture : Lun–Sam 10h–19h | **Le « petit plus »** : C'est dans cette maison que Coco Chanel a ouvert son premier atelier | « La mode passe, le style reste » a dit Coco Chanel – une devise à laquelle on reste fidèle ici depuis 1910. Les tailleurs en tweed et le « Chanel N° 5 » sont légendaires.

Concept Store
Design: Arnaud Montigny (France, 1997)

Open: Mon–Sat 11.00–19.00 | **X-Factor:** Stars such as Karl Lagerfeld and Helena Christensen have exhibitions in the gallery.
Paris' first concept store sells design and life-style articles today which are the trends of tomorrow.

Öffnungszeiten: Mo–Sa 11–19 Uhr | **X-Faktor:** In der Galerie stellen Stars wie Karl Lagerfeld und Helena Christensen aus.
Der erste Concept-Store von Paris verkauft schon heute Design- und Lifestyle-Artikel, die erst morgen Trend sind.

Horaires d'ouverture : Lun–Sam 11h–19h | **Le « petit plus »** : Des stars comme Karl Lagerfeld et Helena Christensen exposent leurs articles dans la galerie.
Le premier concept store de Paris vend aujourd'hui des produits design et lifestyle qui feront la mode de demain.

Comme des Garçons Parfums
23, Place du Marché St-Honoré
75001 Paris
☎ +33 1 47 03 15 03

P. 20/21

Astier de Villatte
173, rue St-Honoré
75001 Paris
☎ +33 1 42 60 74 13
www.astierdevillatte.com

P. 24/25

Avant-garde Perfumes
Design: Façade: Future Systems (UK, 1998) | **Interior:** Rei Kawakubo, Takao Kawasaki

Open: Mon–Sat 11.00–19.00 | **X-Factor:** The perfumed candles named after holy cities.
Rei Kawakubo considers perfumes to be an experimental field and presents them in a futuristic ambience.

Öffnungszeiten: Mo–Sa 11–19 Uhr | **X-Faktor:** Die Duftkerzen, benannt nach heiligen Städten.
Parfums bezeichnet Rei Kawakubo als Experimentierfeld – und präsentiert sie in futuristischem Ambiente.

Horaires d'ouverture : Lun–Sam 11h–19h | **Le « petit plus »** : Les bougies parfumées portant le nom des villes saintes.
Pour Rei Kawakubo, les parfums sont un champ d'expérimentation qu'il présente dans une ambiance futuriste.

White Ceramics
Interior: Rooms in country style

Open: Mon–Sat 11.00–19.30 | **X-Factor:** The series of octagonal crockery named after St. Honoré.
The Astier de Villatte factory is famous for its white-glazed ceramics, many of which recall the France of days gone by.

Öffnungszeiten: Mo–Sa 11–19.30 Uhr | **X-Faktor:** Die achteckige Geschirrlinie, die nach St-Honoré benannt ist.
Die Manufaktur Astier de Villatte ist für weiß lasierte Keramikwaren bekannt – viele erinnern an das Frankreich vergangener Zeiten.

Horaires d'ouverture : Lun–Sam 11h–19h30 | **Le « petit plus »** : La ligne de vaisselle octogonale nommée d'après St-Honoré | La manufacture Astier de Villatte est connue pour ses pièces de céramique émaillées de blanc dont plusieurs évoquent la France de l'ancien temps.

Maison Martin Margiela

25 bis, rue de Montpensier
75001 Paris
☏ +33 1 40 15 07 55
www.maisonmartinmargiela.com

P. 28/29

Pierre Hardy

156, Galerie de Valois
Jardins du Palais Royal
75001 Paris
☏ +33 1 42 60 59 75
www.pierrehardy.com

P. 34/35

Modern Fashion
Design: Studio Margiela (2002 & 2005)

Open: Mon–Sat 11.00–19.00 | **X-Factor:** The "deconstructed" fashion with the seams on the outside. Margiela's trademark is the label without any name, only numbers. Even his boutique is presented without frills.

Öffnungszeiten: Mo–Sa 11–19 Uhr | **X-Faktor:** Die „dekonstruierte" Mode, bei der die Nähte außen liegen. Margielas Markenzeichen ist das namenlose Label, auf dem nur Zahlen stehen. Auch seine Boutique gibt sich schnörkellos.

Horaires d'ouverture : Lun–Sam 11h–19h | **Le « petit plus » :** La mode « déconstruite » où les coutures se trouvent à l'endroit.
La caractéristique de Margiela est son label sans nom qui ne porte que des chiffres. Sa boutique est également très sobre.

High Heels
Design: Pierre Hardy, BP Architectures (France, 2003)

Open: Mon–Sat 11.00–19.00 | **X-Factor:** The new handbags, which have already become collector's items. Pierre Hardy used to be in charge of the shoe page in VOGUE Homme. Today he designs shoes for stars like Nicole Kidman.

Öffnungszeiten: Mo–Sa 11–19 Uhr | **X-Faktor:** Die neuen Handtaschen, die schon Sammlerstücke sind. Bei der VOGUE Homme betreute Pierre Hardy einst die Schuhseite – heute entwirft er Modelle für Stars wie Nicole Kidman.

Horaires d'ouverture : Lun–Sam 11h–19h | **Le « petit plus » :** Les nouveaux sacs qui sont déjà des objets de collection | Pierre Hardy s'est chargé jadis de la page chaussures pour VOGUE Homme. Aujourd'hui, il crée des modèles pour des stars comme Nicole Kidman.

Champs-Élysées
Étoile

Ave. Foch

Rue de la Pompe

Avenue

Ave. Bugeaud

Avenue Victor Hugo

Avenue

M Victor Hugo

Place Victor Hugo

M Kléber

Kléber

Rue Kléber

ARC DE TRIOMPHE

M Charles Ét...

LO VU

Avenue D'Iéna

Avenue

Rue de

GÉOF

Lauriston

Raymond

Rue Boissière

Rue

LA MAISON DE BACCARAT

M Boissière

Avenue

Rue de Lubeck

Ave. d'Iéna

Rue de Chaillot

Avenue Pierre 1er

PALAIS GALLIER

Poincaré

Ave. d'Eylau

Avenue

Rue du

M Iéna

Président Wilson

PALA

Place du Trocadéro et du 11 Novembre

M Trocadéro

MUSÉE DE LA MARINE

JARDINS DU TROCADÉRO

Ave. de New York

Place de Varsovie

Quai Branly

MUSÉE DU QUAI DE BRANLY

PALAIS DE CHAILLOT

HERMÈS
LA MAISON GUERLAIN
LA MAISON DU CHOCOLAT
HÉDIARD
George V
Rue Balzac
Rue Washington
Rue de Berri
Rue du Faubourg St-Honoré
La Boétie
St-Philippe du Roule
Avenue des Champs-Élysées
Rue de Ponthieu
Avenue Franklin D. Roosevelt
Ave. Matignon
Rue Pierre Charron
Rue François 1er
Franklin-D. Roosevelt
Rond-Point des Champs-Élysées
Avenue Montaigne
Avenue George V
R. de Serbie
Marceau
GRAND PALAIS
Alma-Marceau
DE TOKYO
Cours Albert 1er
Cours la Reine
SEINE
Pont de l'Alma
Quai d'orsay
Ave. Rapp
Ave. Bosquet
Rue de l'Université

Hermès

24, rue du Faubourg St-Honoré, 75008 Paris
☎ +33 1 40 17 47 17
www.hermes.com
Métro: Concorde/Madeleine

Comme des Garçons

54, rue du Faubourg St-Honoré, 75008 Paris
☎ +33 1 53 30 27 27
Métro: Concorde/Madeleine

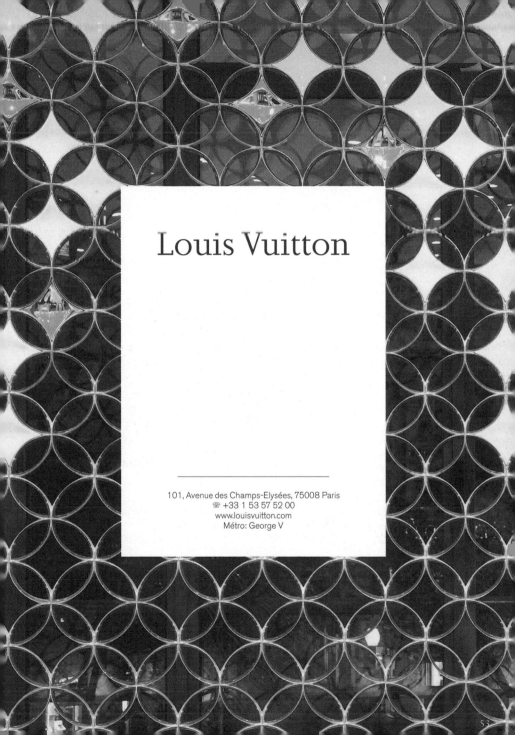

Louis Vuitton

101, Avenue des Champs-Elysées, 75008 Paris
☎ +33 1 53 57 52 00
www.louisvuitton.com
Métro: George V

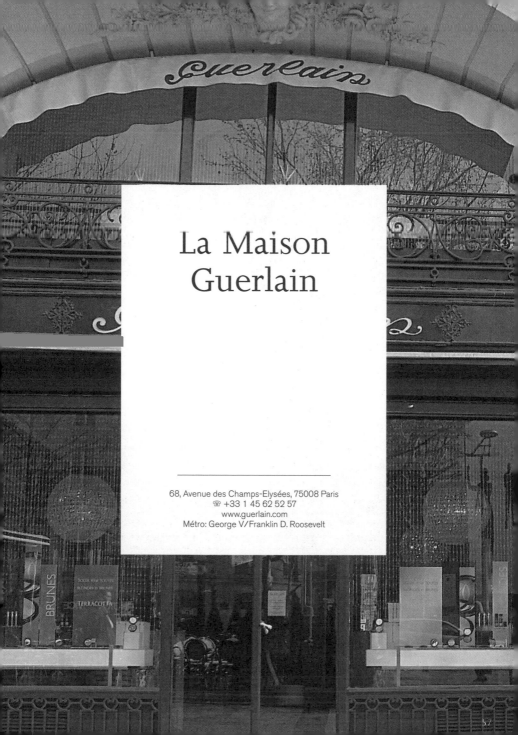

La Maison Guerlain

68, Avenue des Champs-Elysées, 75008 Paris
☎ +33 1 45 62 52 57
www.guerlain.com
Métro: George V/Franklin D. Roosevelt

Hédiard

31, Avenue George V, 75008 Paris
☎ +33 1 47 20 44 44
www.hediard.fr
Métro: George V

THÉ - CAFÉ

La Maison
du Chocolat

52, rue François 1er, 75008 Paris
☎ +33 1 47 23 38 25
www.lamaisonduchocolat.com
Métro: George V

La Maison de Baccarat

11, Place des Etats-Unis, 75116 Paris
☎ +33 1 40 22 11 22
www.baccarat.fr
Métro: Boissière/Kléber

Hermès

24, rue du Faubourg St-Honoré
75008 Paris
☎ +33 1 40 17 47 17
www.hermes.com

P. 44/45

Comme des Garçons

54, rue du Faubourg St-Honoré
75008 Paris
☎ +33 1 53 30 27 27

P. 48/49

Classical Fashion & Leather Goods
Design: Rena Dumas (RDAI, France)

Open: Mon–Sat 10.30–18.30 | **X-Factor:** Classics such as the Birkin Bag or the Kelly Bag. Even celebrities queue up for these.
Here you can find the legends of the label, for example the "Carré Hermès", based on the scarves of Napoleon's soldiers.

Öffnungszeiten: Mo–Sa 10.30–18.30 Uhr | **X-Faktor:** Klassiker wie die Birkin Bag und die Kelly Bag, für die selbst VIPs Schlange stehen.
Hier findet man die Legenden des Labels – etwa das „Carré Hermès", das den Schals von Napoleons Soldaten nachempfunden wurde.

Horaires d'ouverture : Lun–Sam 10h30–18h30 | **Le « petit plus » :** Des classiques comme le sac Birkin ou le sac Kelly pour lesquels même les VIP font la queue | C'est ici qu'on trouve les articles légendaires de la marque, comme le « Carré Hermès » inspiré de l'écharpe que portaient les soldats de Napoléon Ier.

Fashion for Intellectuals
Design: Rei Kawakubo & Takao Kawasaki with Abe Rogers & Shona Kitchen (KRD, UK, 2001)

Open: Mon–Sat 11.00–19.00 | **X-Factor:** The chili-pepper red chill-out lounge.
Rei Kawakubo displays her collection for men and women in award-winning interior design.

Öffnungszeiten: Mo–Sa 11–19 Uhr | **X-Faktor:** Die knall-rote Chill-out-Lounge.
In preisgekröntem Interior Design zeigt Rei Kawakubo ihre Kollektion für Damen und Herren.

Horaires d'ouverture : Lun–Sam 11h–19h | **Le « petit plus » :** Le Chill out-Lounge rouge vif.
Rei Kawakubo présente ses collections pour femmes et pour hommes dans un intérieur design qui a été primé.

Louis Vuitton

101, Avenue des Champs-Elysées
75008 Paris
☎ +33 1 53 57 52 00
www.louisvuitton.com

P. 52/53

La Maison Guerlain

68, Avenue des Champs-Elysées
75008 Paris
☎ +33 1 45 62 52 57
www.guerlain.com

P. 56/57

Luxury Fashion & Leather Goods
Design: Peter Marino and Eric Carlson (USA, 2005)

Open: Mon–Sat 10.00–20.00, Sun 13.00–19.00 | **X-Factor:** The largest Louis Vuitton boutique in the world.
The range in the new Louis Vuitton flagship store is unbeatable, as is the light and sound design by artists such as Olafur Eliasson.

Öffnungszeiten: Mo–Sa 10–20, So 13–19 Uhr | **X-Faktor:** Die größte Louis-Vuitton-Boutique der Welt.
Das Sortiment im neuen LV-Flagshipstore ist unschlagbar – ebenso wie das Licht- und Sounddesign von Künstlern wie Olafur Eliasson.

Horaires d'ouverture : Lun–Sam 10h–20h, Dim 13h–19h | **Le « petit plus » :** La plus grande boutique Louis Vuitton du monde | Le stock du nouveau magasin Louis Vuitton est imbattable, tout comme d'ailleurs le son et lumière d'artistes tel que Olafur Eliasson.

Perfumes & Day Spa
Design: Andrée Putman and Maxime d'Angeac (France, 2005)

Open: Mon–Sat 10.30–20.00, Sun 15.00–19.00 | **X-Factor:** The "Guerlain Impérial" treatment in the new day spa.
All the perfumes in Guerlain's history are available here, including such rarities as "Liu" or "Vega".

Öffnungszeiten: Mo–Sa 10.30–20, So 15–19 Uhr | **X-Faktor:** Die „Guerlain Impérial"-Behandlungen im neuen Day Spa.
Hier findet man alle Parfums der Guerlain-Geschichte – selbst Raritäten wie „Liu" oder „Vega".

Horaires d'ouverture : Lun–Sam 10h30–20h, Dim 15h–19h | **Le « petit plus » :** Les soins « Guerlain Impérial » dans le nouveau Day Spa.
On trouve ici tous les parfums de l'histoire de Guerlain, même les plus rares comme « Liu » ou « Vega ».

Hédiard

31, Avenue George V
75008 Paris
☎ +33 1 47 20 44 44
www.hediard.fr

P. 60/61

La Maison
du Chocolat

52, rue François 1er
75008 Paris
☎ +33 1 47 23 38 25
www.lamaisonduchocolat.com

P. 64/65

Exotic Delicatessen
History: The best delicatessen retailer in Paris since 1854

Open: Mon–Fri 09.00–21.00, Sat/Sun 09.00–20.00 |
X-Factor: The perfect selection of assorted herbs.
The atbouthe thei benou and saaoo In ichila I Idlad pudla
his goods recall the former colonial style store.

Pralinés & Chocolate Tastings
Interior: Completely chocolate brown

Open: Mon–Wed 10.00–19.30, Thurs-Sat 10.00–20.00 |
X-Factor: The chocolate tastings.
Thu hand mudu tuffhan In thu "Manghu d'Ou" nu nlungu woulh
sinning for, and even the display window is a temptation.

Öffnungszeiten: Mo–Fr 9–21, Sa/So 9–20 Uhr | **X-Faktor:**
Die perfekt sortierte Kräuterauswahl.
An das ehemalige Kontor erinnern noch heute die Dosen,
Schachteln und Kisten, in die Hédiard seine Waren stilvoll
verpackt.

Öffnungszeiten: Mo–Mi 10–19.30, Do–Sa 10–20 Uhr |
X-Faktor: Die Schokoladen-Degustationen.
Die handgemachten Trüffel im „Triangle d'Or" sind immer eine
Sünde wert, und auch die Schaufensterdekoration ist zum
Anbeißen.

Horaires d'ouverture : Lun–Ven 9h–21h, Sam/Dim 9h–20h |
Le « petit plus » : Un choix d'épices incomparable.
L'élégant boîtage des produits rappelle aujourd'hui encore
l'ancien comptoir des Épices et des Colonies.

Horaires d'ouverture : Lun–Mer 10h–19h30, Jeu–Sam
10h–20h | **Le « petit plus » :** Les dégustations de chocolat.
On pourrait se damner pour déguster une seule de ces truffes
maison au « Triangle d'Or ». L'eau vient déjà à la bouche rien
qu'en regardant la décoration des vitrines.

La Maison
de Baccarat

11, Place des Etats-Unis
75116 Paris
☎ +33 1 40 22 11 22
www.baccarat.fr

P. 68/69

French Crystal
Design: Philippe Starck (France, 2003)

Open: Mon–Sat: 10.00–21.00 | **X-Factor:** A complete work
of art composed of museum, boutique and restaurant.
Marie-Laure Noailles used to hold her artistic salons in this
villa where Baccarat today directs its empire.

Öffnungszeiten: Mo–Sa 10–21 Uhr | **X-Faktor:** Ein Gesamt-
kunstwerk aus Museum, Boutique und Restaurant.
In dieser Villa lud Marie-Laure Noailles früher zu künstlerischen
Salons – heute besitzt Baccarat hier sein Imperium.

Horaires d'ouverture : Lun–Sam 10h–21h | **Le « petit
plus » :** Une œuvre d'art totale composée d'un musée, d'une
boutique et d'un restaurant.
Marie-Laure Noailles tenait son salon artistique dans cette
maison. Aujourd'hui, Baccarat y dirige son empire.

Rue Marcadet

Rue Ramey

Lamarck-
Caulaincourt Ⓜ

Rue des Saules

SACRÉ
CŒUR

Rue Lamarck

Ave. de Saint-Ouen

Rue Carpeaux

Rue de Damrémont

Rue Joseph de Maistre

Rue Caulaincourt

CIMETIÈRE
DE
MONTMARTRE

Ave. de Clichy

La Fourche Ⓜ

Ave. de Clichy

Rue des Dames

Rue Lepic

Rue Lepic

Rue Tholozé

Rue Durantin

Rue des Trois Frères

Rue des Abbesses

SPREE

Funiculaire

Pl. St-Pierre

TATI →

Bd.
Blanche   Abbesses Ⓜ

Ⓜ Place de
Clichy

de

Ⓜ
Pigalle   Clichy Ⓜ

Bd. de Rochechouart

Anvers Ⓜ

Rue Lepic

Rue Fontaine

Avenue Trudaine

GRANDE
HERBORISTERIE

Rue des Martyrs

Rue de Rochechouart

Liège Ⓜ

Rue d'Amsterdam

Rue de Clichy

Rue Blanche

St-Ⓜ
Georges

Rue de Maubeuge

Rue de Londres

St-
Lazare Ⓜ

St-Lazare

Ⓗ Trinité

Rue de Châteaudun

Ⓜ Cadet

Montmartre
Pigalle

Grande Herboristerie Parisienne de la Place Clichy

87, rue d'Amsterdam, 75008 Paris
☏ +33 1 48 74 83 32
Métro: Place de Clichy/Liège

Spree

16, rue La Vieuville, 75018 Paris
☎ +33 1 42 23 41 40
Métro: Abbesses

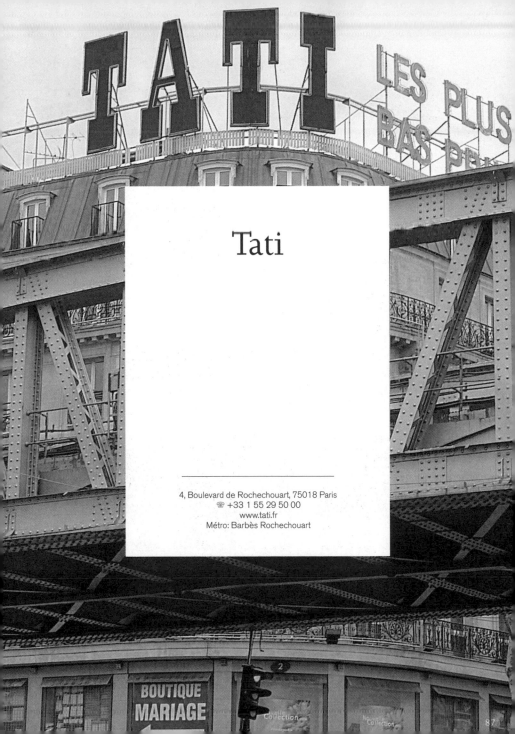

Tati

4, Boulevard de Rochechouart, 75018 Paris
☎ +33 1 55 29 50 00
www.tati.fr
Métro: Barbès Rochechouart

89

Grande Herboristerie Parisienne de la Place Clichy

87, rue d'Amsterdam
75008 Paris
☎ +33 1 48 74 83 32

P. 78/79

Spree

16, rue La Vieuville
75018 Paris
☎ +33 1 42 23 41 40

P. 82/83

Healing Herbs
Interior: Herbal pharmacy in Art Nouveau style

Open: Mon–Sat 10.00–13.00 and 14.00–19.00 (Mon from 11.00, Sat until 18.00) | **X-Factor:** Excellent "infusions" (soothing herbal teas).
At the counter you can choose from more than 900 herbs and can have remedies individually prepared.

Öffnungszeiten: Mo–Sa 10–13 und 14–19 Uhr (Mo ab 11, Sa bis 18 Uhr) | **X-Faktor:** Sehr gute „infusions" (beruhigende Kräutertees).
Am Tresen kann man aus mehr als 900 Kräutern wählen und sich Medizin individuell zusammenstellen lassen.

Horaires d'ouverture : Lun–Sam 10h–13h et 14h–19h (Lun à partir de 11h, Sam jusqu'à 18h) | **Le « petit plus » :** Très bonnes infusions.
Un choix de plus de 900 plantes vous est proposé, des mélanges individuels sont préparés.

Fashion & Furniture
Interior: Designer furniture of the fifties and sixties

Open: Mon–Sat 11.00–19.30, Sun 15.00–19.00 | **X-Factor:** Reasonable prices for unusual furniture.
Even Hollywood stars like Kirsten Dunst love the second-hand atmosphere of the fashion and furniture salesrooms.

Öffnungszeiten: Mo–Sa 11–19.30, So 15–19 Uhr | **X-Faktor:** Annehmbare Preise für außergewöhnliche Modelle.
Die Second-hand-Atmosphäre, in der Mode und Möbel verkauft werden, lieben auch Hollywoodstars wie Kirsten Dunst.

Horaires d'ouverture : Lun–Sam 11h–19h30, Dim 15h–19h | **Le « petit plus » :** Prix acceptables pour des modèles exceptionnels | Les stars d'Hollywood comme Kirsten Dunst aiment aussi cette atmosphère de « seconde main » qui entoure la vente de la mode et des meubles.

Tati

4, Boulevard de Rochechouart
75018 Paris
☎ +33 1 55 29 50 00
www.tati.fr

P. 86/87

Department Store
Interior: A kingdom of rummage tables

Open: Mon–Fri 10.00–19.00, Sat 09.15–19.00 | **X-Factor:** The pink-and-white checked carrier bags.
The best of all places to rummage around in. Tati has attracted bargain hunters for more than 50 years and even has a special department for wedding dresses.

Öffnungszeiten: Mo–Fr 10–19, Sa 9.15–19 Uhr | **X-Faktor:** Die rosa-weiß karierten Tragetaschen.
Nirgendwo sonst ist Stöbern schöner: Das Tati zieht Schnäppchenjäger seit mehr als 50 Jahren an und hat sogar eine extra Abteilung für Brautkleider.

Horaires d'ouverture : Lun–Ven 10h–19h, Sam 9h15–19h | **Le « petit plus » :** Les sacs à carreaux rose et blanc | Nulle part ailleurs on éprouve autant de plaisir à fouiller dans les étals : Tati attire les clients en quête de bonnes affaires depuis plus de 50 ans et possède même un rayon spécial pour les robes de mariée.

Marais
Bastille

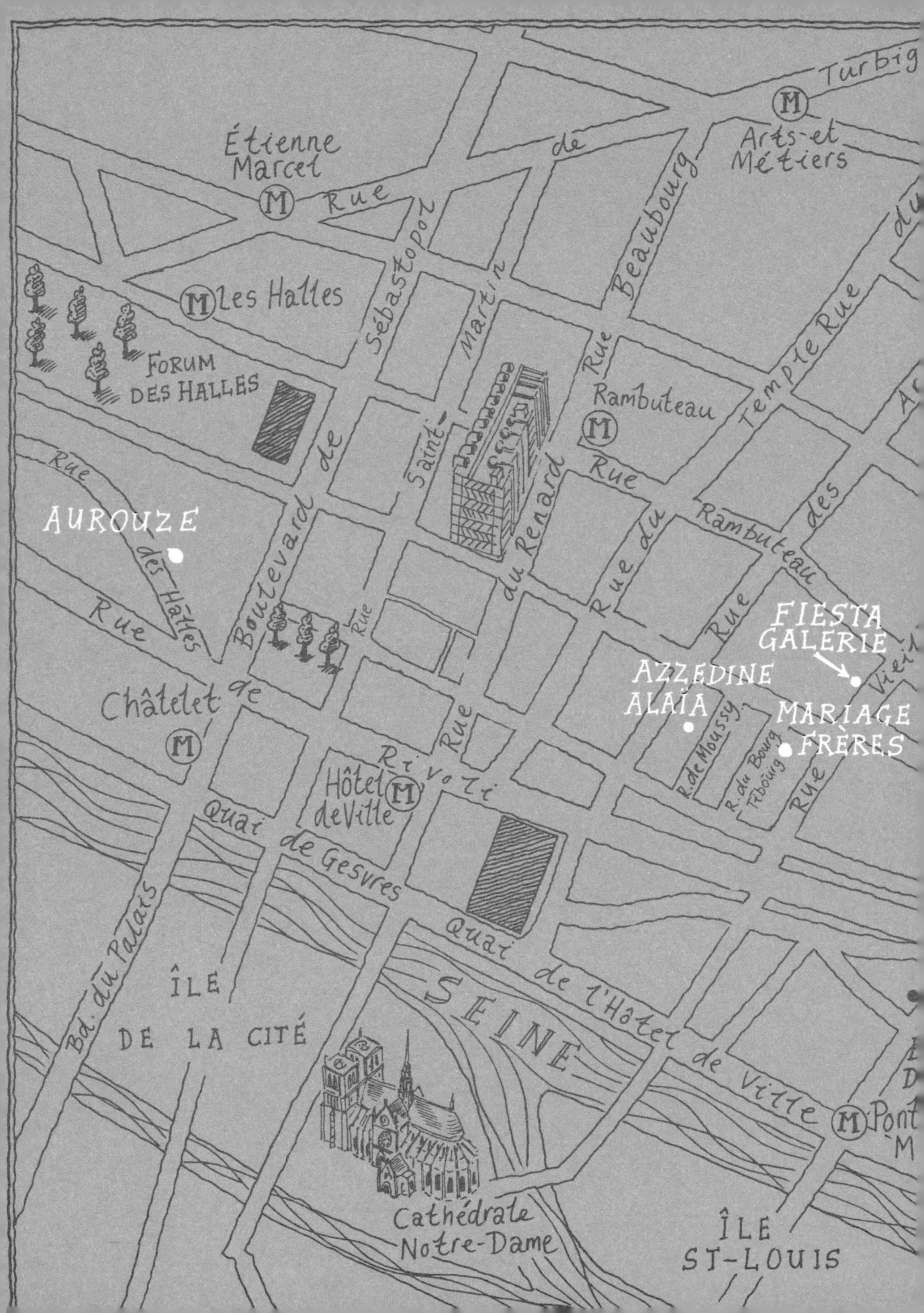
Turbig
Arts-et Métiers
Étienne Marcel
Rue de
Rue Beaubourg
Les Halles
FORUM DES HALLES
Sébastopol
Martin
Saint-
Rue
Rambuteau
Temple
Rue
Rue des
Rue
Boulevard de
du Renard
AUROUZE
Rue des Halles
Rue du
Rue Rambuteau
FIESTA GALERIE
AZZEDINE ALAÏA
MARIAGE FRÈRES
Vieill
Rue
R. de Moussy
R. du Bourg Tibourg
Rue
Châtelet
de
Rue
Rivoli
Hôtel de Ville
Quai de Gesvres
Quai de l'Hôtel de Ville
Bd. du Palais
ÎLE DE LA CITÉ
SEINE
Cathédrale Notre-Dame
ÎLE ST-LOUIS
Pont M

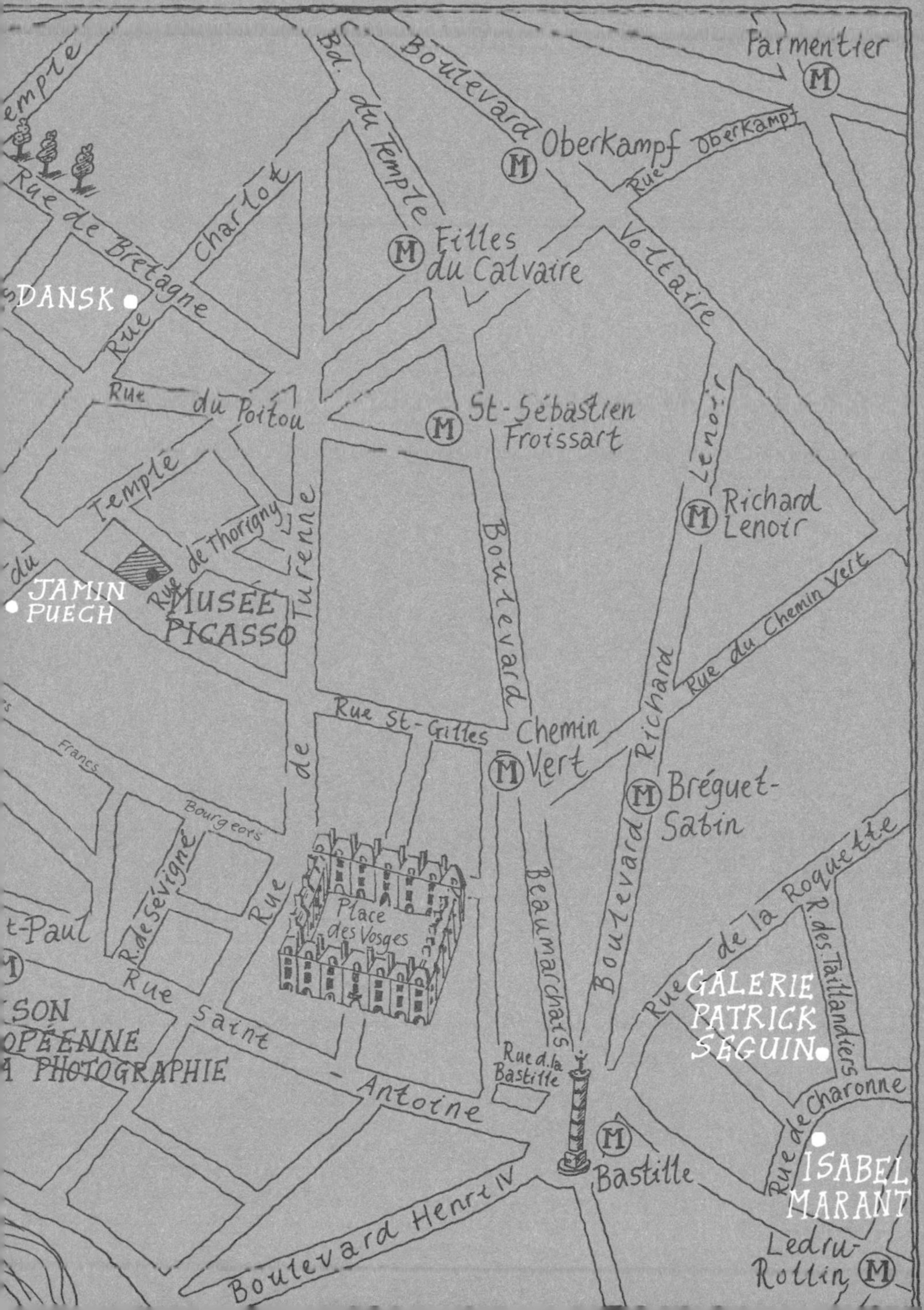
Parmentier
Boulevard Oberkampf
Rue Oberkampf
Bd. du Temple
Temple
Rue de Bretagne
Charlot
Filles du Calvaire
Voltaire
DANSK
Rue
Rue du Poitou
St-Sébastien Froissart
Lenoir
Temple
Richard Lenoir
Rue de Thorigny
du
JAMIN PUECH
MUSÉE PICASSO
Turenne
Boulevard
Rue du Chemin Vert
Francs
Rue St-Gilles
Chemin Vert
de
Richard
Bourgeois
Bréguet-Sabin
R. de Sévigné
Rue
Place des Vosges
Beaumarchais
Boulevard
R. des Taillandiers
de la Roquette
t-Paul
Rue
GALERIE PATRICK SEGUIN
SON
OPÉENNE
A PHOTOGRAPHIE
Rue Saint Antoine
Rue d. la Bastille
Rue de Charonne
Bastille
ISABEL MARANT
Boulevard Henri IV
Ledru-Rollin

Isabel Marant

16, rue de Charonne, 75011 Paris
☎ +33 1 49 29 71 55
Métro: Bastille/Ledru-Rollin

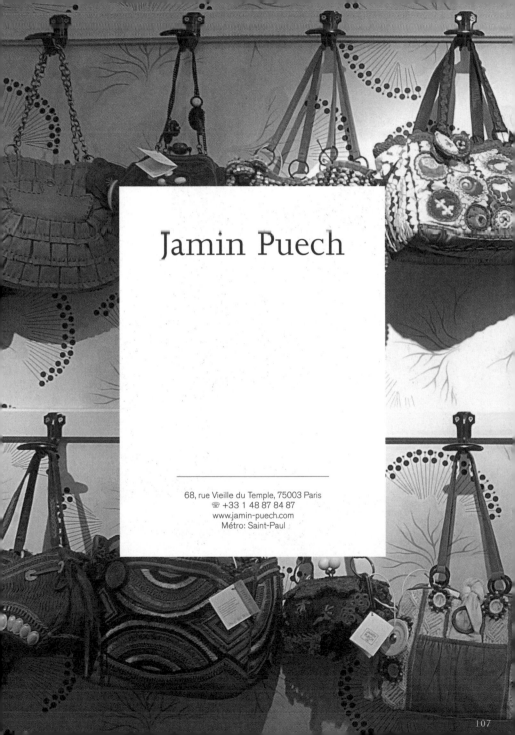

Jamin Puech

68, rue Vieille du Temple, 75003 Paris
☎ +33 1 48 87 84 87
www.jamin-puech.com
Métro: Saint-Paul

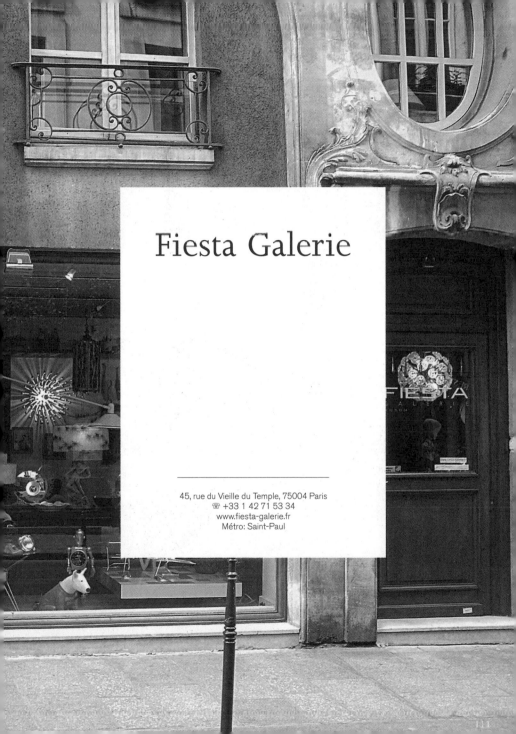

Fiesta Galerie

45, rue du Vieille du Temple, 75004 Paris
☎ +33 1 42 71 53 34
www.fiesta-galerie.fr
Métro: Saint-Paul

Mariage Frères

30/35, rue du Bourg-Tibourg, 75004 Paris
☎ +33 1 42 72 28 11
www.mariagefreres.com
Métro: Saint-Paul

Azzedine Alaïa

7, rue de Moussy, 75004 Paris
☎ +33 1 42 72 19 19
Métro: Saint-Paul

Aurouze

8, rue des Halles, 75001 Paris
☎ +33 1 40 41 16 20
www.aurouze.fr
Métro: Châtelet/Les Halles

Dansk

31, rue Charlot
75003 Paris
☎ +33 1 42 71 45 95
www.galeriedansk.com

P. 96/97

Isabel Marant

16, rue de Charonne
75011 Paris
☎ +33 1 49 29 71 55

P. 100/101

Scandinavian Design
Interior: A living-room with Scandinavian classics

Open: Tues–Sat 14.00–19.00 | **X-Factor:** The design exhibition.
A French-Danish couple has very tastefully arranged designer furniture from the fifties to seventies – from Arne Jacobsen to Verner Panton.

Öffnungszeiten: Di–Sa 14–19 Uhr | **X-Faktor:** Die Designausstellungen.
Ein französisch-dänisches Paar stellt Designermöbel aus den 1950ern bis 1970ern mit viel Geschmack zusammen – von Arne Jacobsen bis zu Verner Panton.

Horaires d'ouverture : Mar–Sam 14h–19h | **Le « petit plus »** : Les expositions de design.
Un couple franco-danois réunit avec beaucoup de goût des meubles design des années 1950 aux années 1970, d'Arne Jacobsen à Verner Panton.

Modern Fashion
Interior: Murals and vintage furniture

Open: Mon–Sat 10.30–19.30 | **X-Factor:** The children's line which has enlarged the portfolio since 2004.
Isabel Marant has been awarded a prize for best designer in France for her very wearable designs with an ethnic touch.

Öffnungszeiten: Mo–Sa 10.30–19.30 Uhr | **X-Faktor:** Die Kinderlinie, die das Portfolio seit 2004 erweitert.
Isabel Marant wurde schon als beste Designerin Frankreichs ausgezeichnet – für ihre immer tragbaren Modelle mit Ethno-Touch.

Horaires d'ouverture : Lun–Sam 10h30–19h30 | **Le « petit plus »** : La ligne enfants élargie depuis 2004 par Portfolio.
Isabel Marant a déjà été nommée meilleure styliste de France pour ses modèles toujours portables avec leur touche ethno.

Jamin Puech

68, rue Vieille du Temple
75003 Paris
☎ +33 1 48 87 84 87
www.jamin-puech.com

P. 106/107

Fiesta Galerie

45, rue du Vieille du Temple
75004 Paris
☎ +33 1 42 71 53 34
www.fiesta-galerie.fr

P. 110/111

Handmade Handbags
Interior: A mixture of styles and colours

Open: Mon–Fri 11.00–19.00 Sat 12.00–19.00 | **X-Factor:** There are more than 100 new designs each year.
Benoît Jamin and Isabelle Puech produce the quirkiest bags in the city and even Karl Lagerfeld has shopped here.

Öffnungszeiten: Mo–Fr 11–19, Sa 12–19 Uhr | **X-Faktor:** Pro Jahr gibt es mehr als 100 neue Designs.
Benoît Jamin und Isabelle Puech stellen die schrägsten Taschen der Stadt her – selbst Karl Lagerfeld war bei ihnen schon Kunde.

Horaires d'ouverture : Lun–Ven 11h–19h, Sam 12h–19h | **Le « petit plus »** : Plus d'une centaine de nouvelles créations par an.
Benoît Jamin et Isabelle Puech proposent les sacs les plus fous de la ville. Ils comptent même Karl Lagerfeld parmi leurs clients.

Retro Design & Curiosities
Interior: Design studio and flea market

Open: Mon–Sat 12.00–19.00, Sun 14.00–19.00 | **X-Factor:** The website, which presents all the exhibits.
Lots of kitsch on show right alongside furniture by Saarinen and Le Corbusier – for example, a rhinestone-covered illuminated mini-version of the Eiffel Tower.

Öffnungszeiten: Mo–Sa 12–19, So 14–19 Uhr | **X-Faktor:** Die Website, die alle Exponate zeigt.
Neben Möbeln von Saarinen und Le Corbusier steht viel Kitsch im Raum – wie eine strassbesetzte illuminierte Mini-Version des Eiffelturms.

Horaires d'ouverture : Lun–Sam 12h–19h, Dim 14h–19h | **Le « petit plus »** : La page web qui montre tous les articles en vente. | Les meubles de Saarinen et de Le Corbusier côtoient aussi du kitch, comme une version miniature de la tour Eiffel garnie de strass.

Mariage Frères

30/35, rue du Bourg-Tibourg
75004 Paris
☎ +33 1 42 72 28 11
www.mariagefreres.com

P. 114/115

Azzedine Alaïa

7, rue de Moussy
75004 Paris
☎ +33 1 42 72 19 19

P. 118/119

Tea Paradise
Interior: Classic colonial atmosphere

Open: Mon–Sun 10.30–19.30 | **X-Factor:** The tea classic "Earl Grey Impérial".
The Mariage family has been one of the tea dynasties in France for 300 years and in 1860 even invented the first tea-chocolate.

Öffnungszeiten: Mo–So 10.30–19.30 Uhr | **X-Faktor:** Der Tee-Klassiker „Earl Grey Impérial".
Seit 300 Jahren gehört die Familie Mariage zu den Tee-Dynastien Frankreichs, 1860 erfand sie sogar die erste Tee-Schokolade.

Horaires d'ouverture : Lun–Dim 10h30–19h30 | **Le « petit plus » :** Le classique « Earl Grey Impérial ».
Mariage Frères fait partie des dynasties du thé depuis trois siècles. En 1860, la maison inventa même le premier chocolat au thé.

Modern Fashion
Design: Julian Schnabel (USA, 1990)

Open: Mon–Sat 10.00–19.00 | **X-Factor:** The new Alaïa shoe boutique next door (Design: Marc Newson).
Azzedine Alaïa's designs for the stars emphasise their figures. Sarah Jessica Parker is one of the biggest fans of his stretch fashion.

Öffnungszeiten: Mo–Sa 10–19 Uhr | **X-Faktor:** Die neue Alaïa-Schuhboutique nebenan (Design: Marc Newson).
Azzedine Alaïa kleidet die Stars figurbetont – zu den größten Fans seiner Stretchmode gehört Sarah Jessica Parker.

Horaires d'ouverture : Lun–Sam 10h–19h | **Le « petit plus » :** La nouvelle boutique de chaussures Alaïa juste à côté (design : Marc Newson).
Azzedine Alaïa sait mettre en valeur la silhouette des stars. Sarah Jessica Parker compte parmi les accros de sa mode stretch.

Aurouze

8, rue des Halles
75001 Paris
☎ +33 1 40 41 16 20
www.aurouze.fr

P. 122/123

Bizarre Showcase
History: The specialist in the fight against vermin since 1872

Open: Mon–Fri 09.00–12.30 and 14.00–18.30, Sat 09.00–12.30 and 14.00–18.00 | **X-Factor:** The stuffed rats in the display window.
Should you need insect spray, mouse traps or even a vermin exterminator, you will be given professional advice here.

Öffnungszeiten: Mo–Fr 9–12.30 und 14–18.30, Sa 9–12.30 und 14–18 Uhr | **X-Faktor:** Die ausgestopften Ratten im Schaufenster.
Wer Mückenspray, Mausefallen oder gar einen Kammerjäger braucht, wird hier perfekt beraten.

Horaires d'ouverture : Lun–Ven 9h–12h30 et 14h–18h30, Sam 9h–12h30 et 14h–18h | **Le « petit plus » :** Les rats empaillés de la vitrine.
Vous êtes ici à la bonne adresse si vous avez besoin d'un insecticide, de pièges à souris ou d'un professionnel en dératisation.

LOUVRE

Rue de Rivoli

Pont Neuf

M

Quai François Mitterrand

SEINE

Quai de la Mégrisserie

Quai Malaquais

Rue Bonaparte

Rue

Pont Neuf

ÎLE DE LA CITÉ

Rue Jacob

Rue de

M Cité

Rue de l'Abbaye

J. LEBLANC ET FILS

PIERRE FREY

LA HUNE

M
St-Germain-dès-Prés

Seine

TASCHEN

R. Saint-André des Arts

M St-Michel

Rue du Four

M Mabillon

Bd. Saint-Germain

Rue Jacques

Rue

Rue St-Sulpice

M Odéon

Rue de l'Odéon

DIPTYQUE

M
St-Sulpice

Rue Bonaparte

Cluny
La Sorbonne

M

MUSÉE NATIONAL
DU MOYEN AGE

Rue de Vaugirard

Rue Guynemer

PALAIS DU
LUXEMBOURG

Saint-Michel

QUARTIER
LATIN

Boulevard

Rue Saint-

JARDIN DU
LUXEMBOURG

PANTHÉON

Quartier Latin
St-Germain

DIPTYQU

Diptyque

34, Boulevard Saint-Germain, 75005 Paris
☏ +33 1 43 26 45 27
www.diptyqueparis.com
Métro: Maubert-Mutualité

133

TASCHEN

2, rue de Buci, 75006 Paris
☎ +33 1 40 51 79 22
www.taschen.com
Métro: Mabillon/Odéon

Huilerie
Artisanale
J. Leblanc et fils

6, rue Jacob, 75006 Paris
☎ +33 1 46 34 61 55
www.huile-leblanc.com
Métro: St-Germain-des-Prés

141

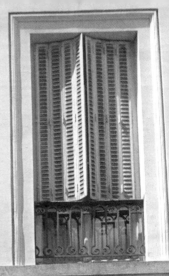

PIERRE FREY

BOUSSAC PIERRE FREY BOUSSAC

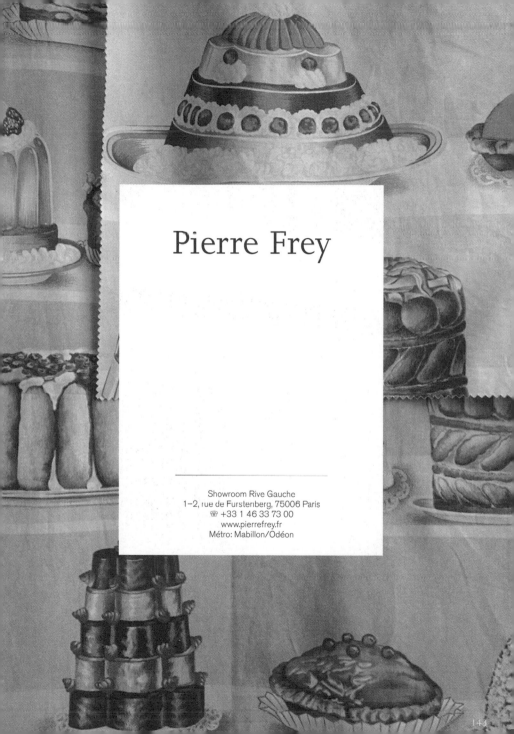

Pierre Frey

Showroom Rive Gauche
1–2, rue de Furstenberg, 75006 Paris
☎ +33 1 46 33 73 00
www.pierrefrey.fr
Métro: Mabillon/Odéon

La Hune

170, Boulevard Saint-Germain, 75006 Paris
☎ +33 1 45 48 35 85
Métro: St. Germain-des-Prés

oderne, contemporain • Photographie
raphisme • Mode • Cuisine • Tourisme
e • Cinéma • Revues art, graphisme,

e :

aise, classique, étrangère • Poésie
ue • Polar • Philosophie • Economie
a • Histoire actualité • Psychanalyse
ologie • Essais Esthétique • Théâtre
ues sciences humaines et littéraires

Diptyque
34, Boulevard Saint-Germain
75005 Paris
+33 1 43 26 45 27
www.diptyqueparis.com

P. 130/131

TASCHEN
2, rue de Buci
75006 Paris
+33 1 40 51 79 22
www.taschen.com

P. 134/135

Scented Perfumes & Candles
History: British perfumes presented as in France

Open: Mon–Sat 10.00–19.00 | **X-Factor:** The small bottles and candles with graphically-designed labels.
Diptyque has been focussing on unusual compositions and candles since 1961. One fragrance was created by John Galliano.

Öffnungszeiten: Mo–Sa 10–19 Uhr | **X-Faktor:** Die Flakons und Kerzen mit grafisch gestalteten Etiketten.
Diptyque setzt seit 1961 auf außergewöhnliche Kompositionen und Kerzen – ein Duft wurde von John Galliano entworfen.

Horaires d'ouverture : Lun–Sam 10h–19h | **Le « petit plus » :** Le dessin des étiquettes apposées sur les flacons et les bougies.
Depuis 1961, Diptyque propose des senteurs et des bougies exceptionnelles. Un parfum a été créé par John Galliano.

Books on Art and Architecture
Design: Philippe Starck (France, 2000)

Open: Mon–Sun 11.00–20.00, Fri/Sat to 00.00 | **X-Factor:** A wide range at a low price.
The complete TASCHEN range is available here on the shelves, as well as extras such as diaries and calendars.

Öffnungszeiten: Mo–So 11–20, Fr/Sa bis 24 Uhr | **X-Faktor:** Das große Angebot zum kleinen Preis.
In den Regalen steht das gesamte TASCHEN-Sortiment – zudem erhält man hier Extras wie Tagebücher und Kalender.

Horaires d'ouverture : Lun–Dim 11h–20h, Ven/Sam jusqu'à 24h | **Le « petit plus » :** Un vaste choix de livres à des prix record.
Vous trouverez ici toutes les collections TASCHEN ainsi que des extras comme les agendas et les calendriers.

Huilerie Artisanale J. Leblanc et fils
6, rue Jacob
75006 Paris
+33 1 46 34 61 55
www.huile-leblanc.com

P. 138/139

Pierre Frey
Showroom Rive Gauche
1–2, rue de Furstenberg
75006 Paris
+33 1 46 33 73 00
www.pierrefrey.fr

P. 142/143

Flavoured Oils & Vinegars
Interior: A shop right out of a children's picture book

Open: Mon 14.00–19.00, Tues–Fri 12.00–19.00, Sat 10.00–19.00 | **X-Factor:** The vinegar and mustard varieties.
The oils have been pressed in a stone mill in Bourgogne since 1878. The nut and pumpkin varieties are in great demand.

Öffnungszeiten: Mo 14–19, Di–Fr 12–19, Sa 10–19 Uhr | **X-Faktor:** Die Essig- und Senfvariationen.
Seit 1878 werden diese Öle in einer Steinmühle in der Bourgogne gepresst; besonders begehrt sind die Sorten Nuss und Kürbis.

Horaires d'ouverture : Lun 14h–19h, Mar–Ven 12h–19h, Sam 10h–19h | **Le « petit plus » :** Les vinaigres et les moutardes.
Depuis 1878, les huiles sont pressées dans une meule de pierre en Bourgogne. L'huile de noix et l'huile de pépins de courge sont particulièrement appréciées.

Fabrics & Home Accessories
History: A fabric empire since 1935

Open: Tues–Sat 10.00–18.30 | **X-Factor:** The wallpapers with their old-French patterns.
Pierre Frey has more than 7,000 fabrics in stock, consequently providing virtually every hotel in Paris with curtains, covers or wallpaper.

Öffnungszeiten: Di–Sa 10–18.30 Uhr | **X-Faktor:** Die Tapeten mit altfranzösischen Mustern.
Pierre Frey hat mehr als 7000 Stoffe im Sortiment – er stattet so gut wie jedes Hotel in Paris mit Vorhängen, Decken oder Tapeten aus.

Horaires d'ouverture : Mar–Sam 10h–18h30 | **Le « petit plus » :** La tapisserie aux motifs Vieille France.
Pierre Frey propose plus de 7000 tissus. Les rideaux, plafonds et tapisseries de la plupart des hôtels parisiens viennent de chez lui.

La Hune

170, Boulevard Saint-Germain
75006 Paris
☎ +33 1 45 48 35 85

P. 146/147

French Literature
History: One of the best addresses for literature in Paris
since 1949

Open: Mon–Sat 10.00–00.00, Sun 11.00–20.00 | **X-Factor:**
The readings by French authors.
Over two floors, every square metre is exploited to present
French classics and art books.

Öffnungszeiten: Mo–Sa 10–24, So 11–20 Uhr | **X-Faktor:**
Die Lesungen französischer Autoren.
Auf zwei Etagen wird jeder Quadratmeter genutzt, um französische Klassiker und Kunstbücher anzubieten.

Horaires d'ouverture : Lun–Sam 10h–24h, Dim 11h–20h |
Le « petit plus » : Les lectures organisées par des auteurs
français.
Deux étages entièrement consacrés aux classiques et livres
d'art français.

Rue de Verneuil

Rue de l'Université

Rue des St-Pères

Quai de Conti

SEINE

Boulevard

CHOCOLAT
DEBAUVE &
GALLAIS

Rue des

Rue

Jacob

Rue de Seine

Rue Mazarine

Boulevard

ST-GERMAIN
DES-PRÉS

Y's YOHJI
YAMAMOTO

R. des Saints-Pères

Rue du Dragon

Saint-

Mabillon

Germain

Odéon

SABBIA ROSA

St-Germain-
des-Prés

M St-Germain
des-Prés

Sèvres
Babylone

Rue de

Sèvres

Sèvres

M

Rue du Cherche-Midi

M ANNICK
GOUTAL

Rue de l'Odéon

M

POILÂNE

Raspail

Rue de Rennes

Pl. St-
Sulpice

St-
Sulpice

✝ ÉGLISE SAINT-SULPICE

Rue de Mézières

Vaugirard

M Rennes

Rue de

Madame

Rue Guynemer

PALAIS DU
LUXEMBOURG

Rue de Fleurus

Rue de Rennes

St- M
Placide

Rue Vavin

Rue d'Assas

JARDIN DU
LUXEMBOURG

Bd. Saint-Michel

Notre-Dame
des Champs M

Rue Auguste Comte

Bd. du Montparnasse

M Vavin

St-Sulpice
Sèvres-Babylone

Chocolat
Debauve & Gallais

30, rue des Saints-Pères, 75007 Paris
☎ +33 1 45 48 54 67
www.debauve-et-gallais.com
Métro: St. Germain-des-Prés

Y's Yohji Yamamoto

69, rue des Saints-Pères, 75006 Paris
☏ +33 1 45 48 22 56
www.yohjiyamamoto.co.jp
Métro: St. Germain-des-Prés

Sabbia Rosa

71–73, rue des Saints-Pères, 75006 Paris
☏ +33 1 45 48 88 37
Métro: Sèvres-Babylone

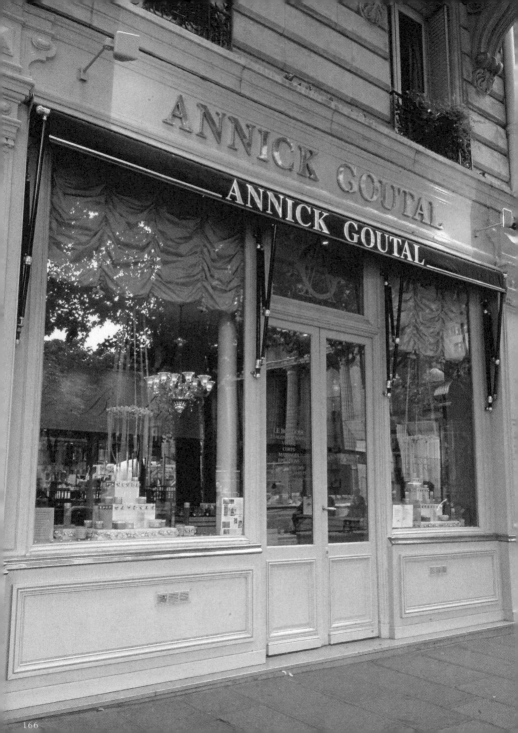

Annick Goutal

12, Place Saint-Sulpice, 75006 Paris
☎ +33 1 46 33 03 15
www.annickgoutal.fr
Métro: Saint-Sulpice/Mabillon/Odéon

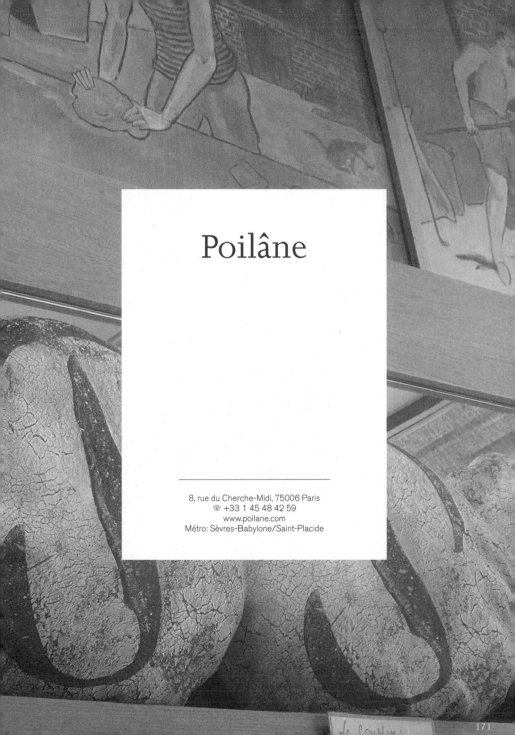

Poilâne

8, rue du Cherche-Midi, 75006 Paris
☎ +33 1 45 48 42 59
www.poilane.com
Métro: Sèvres-Babylone/Saint-Placide

Chocolat Debauve & Gallais

30, rue des Saints-Pères
75007 Paris
☏ +33 1 45 48 54 67
www.debauve-et-gallais.com

P. 154/155

Y's Yohji Yamamoto

69, rue des Saints-Pères
75006 Paris
☏ +33 1 45 48 22 56
www.yohjiyamamoto.co.jp

P. 158/159

Traditional Dark Chocolates
Design: Built by Napoleon's architects Percier & Fontaine (1819)

Open: Mon–Sat 09.30–19.00 | **X-Factor:** The classic boxes with the seal emblem.
Not only Marie-Antoinette but also Balzac and Proust became weak at the thought of these chocolates.

Öffnungszeiten: Mo–Sa 9.30–19 Uhr | **X-Faktor:** Die klassischen Kartons mit Siegel-Emblem.
Beim Genuss dieser dunklen Pralinen schmolzen schon Marie-Antoinette sowie Balzac und Proust dahin.

Horaires d'ouverture : Lun–Sam 9h30–19h | **Le « petit plus » :** Les boîtes avec leur emblème.
Ces délicieux chocolats noirs faisaient déjà les délices de Marie-Antoinette, de Balzac et de Proust.

Asian-inspired Fashion
Interior: Reduced atelier atmosphere

Open: Mon–Sat 10.30–19.00 | **X-Factor:** The accommodating assistance.
The dark façade may appear somewhat intimidating, but whoever goes into the boutique could purchase just about the entire Yamamoto young collection.

Öffnungszeiten: Mo–Sa 10.30–19 Uhr | **X-Faktor:** Die zuvorkommende Beratung.
Die dunkle Fassade wirkt etwas einschüchternd – doch wer die Boutique betritt, kann fast die komplette junge Kollektion von Yamamoto erstehen.

Horaires d'ouverture : Lun–Sam 10h30–19h | **Le « petit plus » :** L'excellent service.
La façade sombre semble un peu intimidante, mais en entrant dans la boutique, on découvre la quasi-totalité de la jeune collection de Yamamoto.

Sabbia Rosa

71–73, rue des Saints-Pères
75006 Paris
☏ +33 1 45 48 88 37

P. 162/163

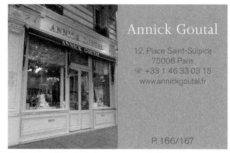

Annick Goutal

12, Place Saint-Sulpice
75006 Paris
☏ +33 1 46 33 03 15
www.annickgoutal.fr

P. 166/167

French Dessous
Interior: Boutique as a boudoir

Open: Mon–Sat 10.00–19.00 | **X-Factor:** Underwear in every possible pastel colour.
Only those who ring the bell gain access to the most elegant dessous in Paris: "Sonnez, s.v.p." is printed next to the doorknob – and even Madonna did.

Öffnungszeiten: Mo–Sa 10–19 Uhr | **X-Faktor:** Wäsche in allen erdenklichen Pastelltönen.
Die elegantesten Dessous von Paris erhält nur, wer klingelt: „Sonnez, s.v.p." steht neben dem Knopf an der Tür – daran hielt sich auch Madonna.

Horaires d'ouverture : Lun–Sam 10h–19h | **Le « petit plus » :** De la lingerie dans tous les tons pastel imaginables.
Si vous voulez obtenir les dessous les plus élégants de Paris, vous devrez d'abord sonner à la porte. Madonna a dû se plier aussi à ce rituel.

Perfumes & Beauty Salon
Interior: Perfumery and beauty salon in delicate pink

Open: Mon–Sat 10.00–19.00 | **X-Factor:** The rose-oil facials in the beauty salon.
Annick Goutal was inspired in Grasse, the city of perfumes, and her heirs sell her fragrances in "Boules Papillon", small bottles with a butterfly stopper.

Öffnungszeiten: Mo–Sa 10–19 Uhr | **X-Faktor:** Die Rosenöl-Facials im Beautysalon.
Annick Goutal ließ sich in Grasse inspirieren – ihre Erbinnen verkaufen ihre Düfte in „Boules Papillon"-Flakons mit Schmetterlings-Verschluss.

Horaires d'ouverture : Lun–Sam 10h–19h | **Le « petit plus » :** Les Facials aux essences de rose dans le salon de beauté.
Annick Goutal a trouvé son inspiration à Grasse. Ses héritières vendent ses senteurs dans des flacons « boules papillon », dont le bouchon est en forme de papillon.

Poilâne
8, rue du Cherche-Midi
75006 Paris
☎ +33 1 45 48 42 59
www.poilane.com

P. 170/171

Traditional French Bakery
History: Family business since 1932

Open: Mon–Sat 07.15–20.15 | **X-Factor:** Pastries with white and dark flour | No credit cards.
You can bake the famous "Pain Poilâne" yourself when the shop is closed on Sunday as the flour and cookery books can be bought here, too.

Öffnungszeiten: Mo–Sa 7.15–20.15 Uhr | **X-Faktor:** Gebäck aus hellem und dunklem Mehl | Keine Kreditkarten.
Wenn am Sonntag geschlossen ist, kann man das berühmte „Pain Poilâne" selbst herstellen: Hier gibt es auch Mehl und Backbücher.

Horaires d'ouverture : Lun–Sam 7h15–20h15 | **Le « petit plus » :** Farine de froment et de blé d'épeautre | Cartes de crédit non acceptées | Le dimanche étant le jour de fermeture, faites vous-même le célèbre « Pain Poilâne ». Vous trouverez dans la boutique la farine et la recette.

Quai des Tuileries

Quai Anatole France

JARDIN DES TUILERIES

JARDIN DU CARROUSEL

Assemblée Nationale Ⓜ

Boulevard

MUSÉE D'ORSAY

Pont Royal

SEINE

Rue de Lille

Rue de Bac

Quai Voltaire

Solférino Ⓜ

Rue

Rue de

●ANDROUËT

de Verneuil

Rue de Montalembert

R.d.St-Simon

Rue du Bac Ⓜ

Rue de Montalembert

LUCIEN ○PELLAT-FINET

●LE MUR DE GAINSBOURG

l'Université

Rue du Bac

Saint-

Germain

St-Germain des-Prés Ⓜ

MUSÉE MAILLOL ●

Rue de

Boulevard

Bac

de

Varenne

CHRISTIAN ○LOUBOUTIN

Grenelle

Rennes

du Four

Rue de Babylone

Rue du

Raspail

Rue de

Sèvres

Sèvres Babylone Ⓜ

Rue de Ⓜ

Saint-Sulpice

Musée d'Orsay
Rue du Bac

178

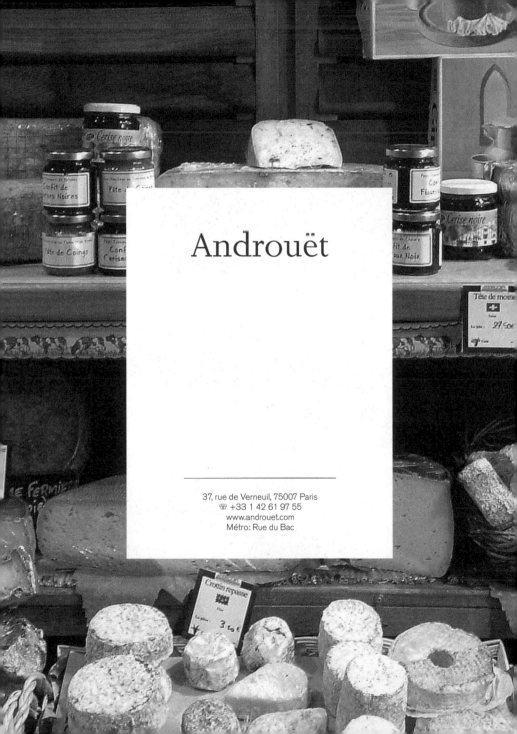

Androuët

37, rue de Verneuil, 75007 Paris
☎ +33 1 42 61 97 55
www.androuet.com
Métro: Rue du Bac

Lucien Pellat-Finet

1, rue de Montalembert, 75007 Paris
☎ +33 1 42 22 22 77
www.lucienpellat-finet.com
Métro: Rue du Bac

Christian Louboutin

38–40, rue de Grenelle, 75007 Paris
☎ +33 1 42 22 33 07
www.christianlouboutin.fr
Métro: Sèvres-Babylone/Rue du Bac

Androuët

37, rue de Verneuil
75007 Paris
☎ +33 1 42 61 97 55
www.androuet.com

P. 178/179

Lucien Pellat-Finet

1, rue de Montalembert
75007 Paris
☎ +33 1 42 22 22 77
www.lucienpellat-finet.com

P. 182/183

Raw-milk Cheese
History: Cheese experts in Paris since 1909

Open: Mon 16.00–19.30, Tues–Sat 09.00–13.00 and 16.00–19.30, Sun 09.00–13.00 | **X-Factor:** The fitting wine for each cheese.
Ernest Hemingway and Maria Callas chose their favourite French raw milk cheese at Androuët's.

Öffnungszeiten: Mo 16–19.30, Di-Sa 9–13 und 16–19.30, So 9–13 Uhr | **X-Faktor:** Die passenden Weine zu jedem Käse.
Bei Androuët suchten sich schon Ernest Hemingway und Maria Callas ihre Lieblingskäse aus französischer Rohmilch aus.

Horaires d'ouverture : Lun 16h–19h30, Mar–Sam 9h–13h et 16h–19h30, Dim 9h–13h | **Le « petit plus » :** Choix de vins qui accompagnent les fromages.
Ernest Hemingway et Maria Callas venaient déjà acheté leur fromage favori chez Androuët.

Cashmere Streetwear
Interior: Minimalist design with touches of colour

Open: Mon–Fri 10.00–19.00, Sat 11.00–19.00 | **X-Factor:** The jeans with ten percent cashmere, and pullovers with patterns by Takashi Murakami.
Lucien Pellat-Finet designs cashmere fashion with patterns such as skulls or hemp leaves, and similarly patterned belts.

Öffnungszeiten: Mo–Fr 10–19 Uhr, Sa 11–19 Uhr | **X-Faktor:** Die Jeans mit zehn Prozent Kaschmiranteil und Pullover mit Motiven von Takashi Murakami.
Lucien Pellat-Finet entwirft Kaschmirmode mit Motiven wie Totenköpfen oder Hanfblättern – und ebenso gemusterte Gürtel.

Horaires d'ouverture : Lun–Ven 10h–19h, Sam 11h–19h | **Le « petit plus » :** Jeans avec 10 % de cachemire et pulls aux dessins de Takashi Murakami | Lucien Pellat-Finet créé une mode en cachemire avec des motifs tels que des têtes de mort ou des feuilles de chanvre, les ceintures sont assorties.

Christian Louboutin

38–40, rue de Grenelle
75007 Paris
☎ +33 1 42 22 33 07
www.christianlouboutin.fr

P. 186/187

Shoes for Stars
Interior: Like a museum with red alcoves for display

Open: Mon–Sat 10.30–19.00 | **X-Factor:** The black peep-toes which have achieved cult status.
Half of Hollywood sashays around on these shoes with the red soles. No other pair of high heels confers such sex appeal.

Öffnungszeiten: Mo–Sa 10.30–19 Uhr | **X-Faktor:** Die schwarzen Peep-Toes mit Kultstatus.
Auf diesen Schuhen mit roten Sohlen schwebt halb Hollywood, denn kein anderes Paar Pumps verleiht mehr Sex-Appeal.

Horaires d'ouverture : Lun–Sam 10h30–19h | **Le « petit plus » :** Les Peep-Toes noires devenues culte.
À Hollywood la moitié des femmes portent ces chaussures à semelle rouge, car elles sont les seules à donner autant de sex-appeal.

© 2007 TASCHEN GmbH
Hohenzollernring 53, D-50672 Köln
www.taschen.com

© 2006 Cover by Olaf Hajek, Berlin
© 2006 Maps by Michael A Hill/Mapsillustrated.com

Compilation, Editing & Layout by
Angelika Taschen, Berlin

Photos by
Vincent Knapp, Paris

General Project Manager
Stephanie Bischoff, Cologne

Design
Eggers + Diaper, Berlin

Lithograph Manager
Thomas Grell, Cologne

German Text Editing
Christiane Reiter, Hamburg

French Translation
Thérèse Chatelain-Südkamp, Cologne

English Translation
Kate Chapman, Berlin

Printed in Italy
ISBN 978-3-8228-4273-7

To stay informed about upcoming TASCHEN titles, please request our
magazine at www.taschen.com/magazine or write to TASCHEN,
Hohenzollernring 53, D-50672 Cologne, Germany, contact@taschen.com,
Fax: +49 221 254919. We will be happy to send you a free copy of our
magazine which is filled with information about all our books.